Moons

by Harriet Loy
Illustrated by Natalya Karpova

BLASTOFF!
MISSIONS

BELLWETHER MEDIA
MINNEAPOLIS, MN

T0014792

Blastoff! Missions takes you on a learning adventure! Colorful illustrations and exciting narratives highlight cool facts about our world and beyond. Read the mission goals and follow the narrative to gain knowledge, build reading skills, and have fun!

BLASTOFF! MISSIONS

Traditional Nonfiction

BLASTOFF! READERS

BLASTOFF! Beginners

BLASTOFF! DISCOVERY

BLASTOFF! MISSIONS

Narrative Nonfiction

Blastoff! Universe

MISSION GOALS

> FIND YOUR SIGHT WORDS IN THE BOOK.

> PICK A MOON THAT YOU WOULD LIKE TO LEARN MORE ABOUT.

> LEARN THE NAMES OF SOME MOONS IN OUR SOLAR SYSTEM.

This edition first published in 2023 by Bellwether Media, Inc.

No part of this publication may be reproduced in whole or in part without written permission of the publisher. For information regarding permission, write to Bellwether Media, Inc., Attention: Permissions Department, 6012 Blue Circle Drive, Minnetonka, MN 55343.

Library of Congress Cataloging-in-Publication Data

Names: Loy, Harriet, author.
Title: Moons / by Harriet Loy.
Description: Minneapolis, MN : Bellwether Media, 2023. | Series: Blastoff! missions. Journey into space | Includes bibliographical references and index. | Audience: Ages 5-8 | Audience: Grades 2-3 |
Summary: "Vibrant illustrations accompany information about various moons in the solar system. The narrative nonfiction text is intended for students in kindergarten through third grade"-- Provided by publisher.
Identifiers: LCCN 2022006866 (print) | LCCN 2022006867 (ebook) | ISBN 9781644876565 (library binding) | ISBN 9781648348402 (paperback) | ISBN 9781648347023 (ebook)
Subjects: LCSH: Satellites--Juvenile literature.
Classification: LCC QB401.5 .L69 2023 (print) | LCC QB401.5° (ebook) | DDC 523.9/8--dc23/eng20220422
LC record available at https://lccn.loc.gov/2022006866
LC ebook record available at https://lccn.loc.gov/2022006867

Text copyright © 2023 by Bellwether Media, Inc. BLASTOFF! MISSIONS and associated logos are trademarks and/or registered trademarks of Bellwether Media, Inc.

Editor: Besty Rathburn   Designer: Jeffrey Kollock

Printed in the United States of America, North Mankato, MN.

This is **Blastoff Jimmy**! He is here to help you on your mission and share fun facts along the way!

Table of Contents

Earth's Moon

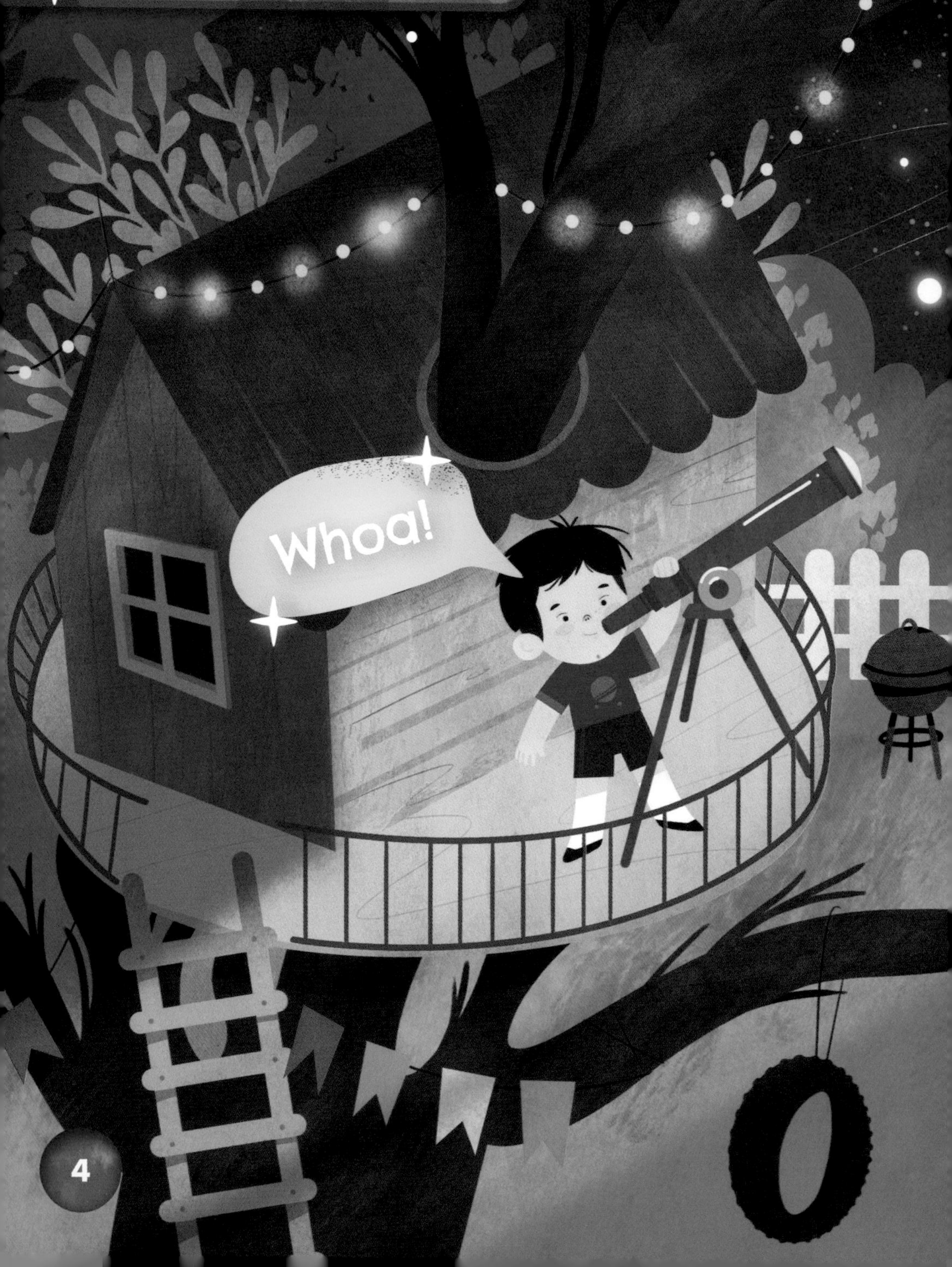

crater

It is a clear, cool night. You look up at the Moon from your backyard. Looking closely, you can see its many **craters** and shades of gray.

Earth's Moon is the largest and brightest body in the night sky. Like all moons, it **orbits** another object.

▶ JIMMY SAYS ◀

Our solar system has over 200 moons. Planets, dwarf planets, and even asteroids have moons!

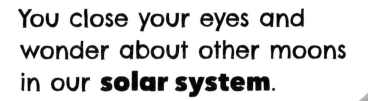

You close your eyes and wonder about other moons in our **solar system**.

Mars is the first stop on your trip. Phobos is the Red Planet's largest moon. It is shaped like a potato and has many craters. It orbits Mars three times in one day!

Cool!

Phobos

Mars

aurora

Ganymede

You travel a long way to Jupiter. This planet has over 75 moons! Ganymede is the largest moon in the solar system.

Colorful **auroras** swirl above its icy surface.

JIMMY SAYS

Scientists think Ganymede has an underground ocean. Moving auroras helped them discover it!

Jupiter

Look out! Another of Jupiter's moons flies past you. It is Io! On its surface, you see hundreds of **volcanoes**. They shoot **lava** thousands of feet into the air!

Io

Yikes!

Saturn

Titan

You zoom to Saturn and see more than 80 moons! A large one stands out to you. Below a thick **atmosphere**, you see rivers and lakes of **methane**. This is Titan!

Miranda and Triton

Uranus

Past Saturn, you see Uranus. It has 27 moons. Your eyes are drawn to one with an odd look. It is Miranda.

Miranda

canyons

Canyons carve deep lines in its surface. They are deeper than any on Earth!

Neptune

You shield your eyes as you near Neptune and its 14 moons. Triton shines brightly in front of you. Sunlight bounces off of the ice covering this cold moon!

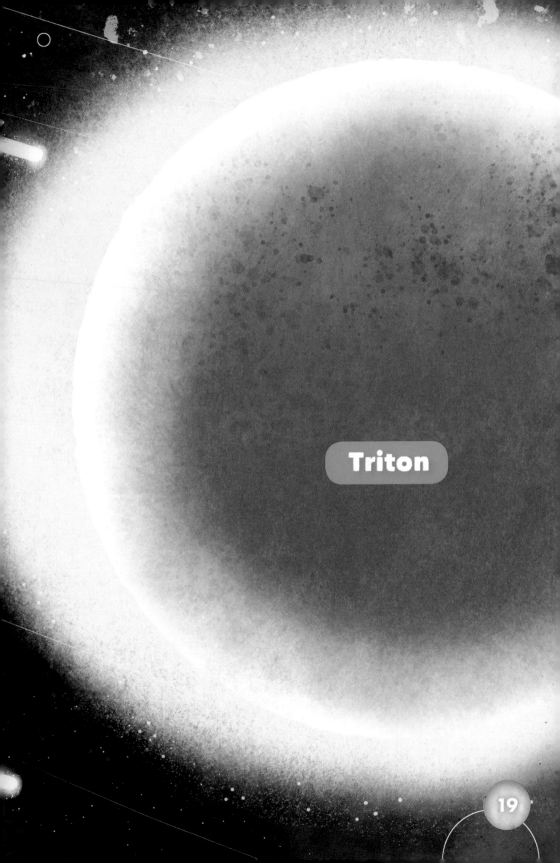

Triton

You open your eyes and your journey ends. Earth's Moon comes back into focus. What other moons would you like to explore?

Moons

Features: brightest in the sky, craters

Orbits: Earth

The Moon

Features: potato shape, fast orbit

Orbits: Mars

Phobos

Features: largest in solar system, auroras

Orbits: Jupiter

Ganymede

Features: volcanoes

Orbits: Jupiter

Io

Features: rivers and lakes of methane

Orbits: Saturn

Titan

Features: deep canyons

Orbits: Uranus

Miranda

Features: icy surface, cold

Orbits: Neptune

Triton

Glossary

atmosphere–the gases that surround a planet or moon

auroras–colorful lights that appear in the atmosphere of a planet or moon; on Earth, auroras are also called northern and southern lights.

canyons–deep, narrow valleys with steep sides

craters–holes in the surface of an object

lava–melted rock

methane–a material which exists as a gas on Earth; methane becomes a liquid in extremely cold places.

orbits–moves in a fixed path around something; all moons orbit another object.

solar system–the group of planets, moons, asteroids, and other bodies that circle around the Sun

volcanoes–holes in the ground; when a volcano erupts, hot ash, gas, or melted rock called lava shoots out.

To Learn More

AT THE LIBRARY

Betts, Bruce. *Super Cool Space Facts: A Fun, Fact-filled Space Book for Kids.* Emeryville, Calif.: Rockridge Press, 2019.

Leaf, Christina. *The Outer Planets.* Minneapolis, Minn.: Bellwether Media, 2023.

McAnulty, Stacy. *Moon!: Earth's Best Friend.* New York, N.Y.: Henry Holt and Company, 2019.

ON THE WEB

FACTSURFER

Factsurfer.com gives you a safe, fun way to find more information.

1. Go to www.factsurfer.com.

2. Enter "moons" into the search box and click 🔍.

3. Select your book cover to see a list of related content.

BEYOND THE MISSION

> CREATE A MOON. WHICH PLANET DOES IT ORBIT? WHAT IS IT LIKE? DRAW A PICTURE.

> WHICH MOON IN THE BOOK WOULD YOU LIKE TO VISIT? WHY?

> WOULD YOU LIKE TO VISIT EARTH'S MOON? WHY OR WHY NOT?

Index